Just Labor

**Also by Laura-Gray Street**

*Pigment and Fume*
*Shift Work* (chapbook)

# JUST LABOR

POEMS

# LAURA-GRAY STREET

Press 53
Winston-Salem

Press 53, LLC
PO Box 30314
Winston-Salem, NC 27130


First Edition

Silver Concho Poetry Series
edited by Pamela Uschuk & Wiliam Pitt Root

Library of Congress Control Number
2025933385


ISBN 978-1-950413-96-6

*for the workers of the world*

# Contents

# IV.

# Drawing In

# Introduction

In this remarkable collection, *Just Labor*, Laura-Gray Street both moves the reader emotionally and provokes her to deeper investigation and understanding. These poems are neither easy nor difficult, each a corporeal entity intimately connected to all the rest. A single working body, if you will. They are the mingling of many voices—mostly those of women—many energies and circumstances, all tapping into the theme of hard work and its multiple consequences in the lives we live. Compassion minus the sentimentality. Metaphor so embedded that it sneaks up on you as insight. The people, the characters, are portrayed with such subtle irony they become truly human before your eyes.

These poems reveal the beleaguered bodies of women who work at home to rear their children and in the mill to raise cloth (or clothes, or tampons) out of cotton. The machines themselves are described in such taut, vivid detail that they too almost come to life. Even the cotton takes on living form. And just when you've got the book figured out, a voice arises to lay down some fast-talking, socio/political wit that makes your head spin faster than a bobbin—the maimings, the deaths, the violence resulting from union strikes, the bloated lives of mill owners.

There are many poems in this collection that will slay you—and not gently—then make you beg for more, that will break your heart, reveal some necessary but difficult truth at the core of who and what we are, and otherwise wake you up from the stupor of your daily trance. Mingling the language of the cotton mill and its machines with the language of desperate love and longing, Street reveals the harsh yet beautiful lives of women working in the unjust conditions of the mills, the earthy ebb and flow of their exhausted bodies.

This is just some of the best damn writing I've encountered anywhere. The language throughout is simultaneously compressed and sharp, cutting and repairing as it goes. But we will never completely heal from the images and stories of this amazing collection. Nor should we.

—Jim Peterson
author of *Towheaded Stone Thrower*

# Finishing

*—converting raw or gray cloth into usable material*

## World Organization of Textiles, or Servo-Mechanical Utopia

Fully automated, the factory becomes a source
of contemplation. Observe how the ceilings are
limitless and machines stretch for miles—
this one blowing up cotton bits to start them
frolicking like dandelion fluff or the effervescent
plastic balls once used for bingo and lotteries,
another skimming eggshell-thin layers from vast
open ranges of bales to blend them. How tenderly
the motorized forklifts scoop and cradle infant
fiber, trundle it to the mothering machines
humming as they spin. Radiant conveyor belts
merry-go-round freshly finished cloth
to schoolyards for packaging and shipping.
Forty times an hour, the air is rinsed of residual
contaminants—sweat, sickness, human history—
and flushed as purified liquid over canyons
of wall fountains that pour into distant oceans
of reflecting pools that reflect only the smoothest
weave of featureless beauty, still, undisturbed.
Think of the endless ways we are relieved.

I.

# Engineering Report

The mechanisms of factory: tower, fire
doors, metal seals, surfaced roofs, brick
facades, arched windows, ventilation
shafts, beams of light as scaffolding . . .

And the cost of each will be used to . . .
And the cost of each will be activated . . .

Prolonged structural issues—
               So long, structure—

Framework thick with façade—
                 Façade is frame—

Windows conspire with space—
                       Space lights desire—

Dust shafts clogged, unmaintained—
                       Dust remains—

Oil and grease fuel further fire—
               Further proof—

Fire doors seal off escape—
               All fire escapes—

And the cost of each prevents further . . .
And the cost of each maintains . . .

In the mill, on the south corner of the lot,
thick structures of memory sealed off by
fire: a locked safe with no combination;
a long, dark tunnel; a darker basement . . .

# Invocation with Textile Mill Workers, Grandmothers, Fates, Quarreling Inner Voices, and Others

How to begin? —Aim spit-stiffened thread
at needle's eye. Or wrap forefinger
with thread ends, roll them, pull off
the knot. —*Now creeling, you tie threads*
*on at the back and run it up on the warps.*
*First job I ever done.* —Blunt-cut with scissors.
Or with your teeth snap thread to ragged
edge, leaving snagged wisps in your mouth.
—Nothing to tell without a story. Without
a clue, or *cliwen,* ball of yarn. —So start
further back, fireside. Comb raw fibers,
twist them to yarn, wrap yarn
onto skein, run skein onto bobbin.
—*Thought is thread, the poet is weaver.*
*Early scribes penned such even, flexible*
*texture they called the page a* textus,
*which means cloth.* —Wale, woof, weave,
weeds. —*The better your yarn, the higher*
*your production.* —Always loose ends,
fraying, frazzling, unraveling. —Can't make
sense of the patterns, those dingy tissue-
thin diagrams that never pin the right
conclusion: dress, skirt, smock. —Then
fabricate. Fit pattern to purpose. —*Work*
*the warp mills, wind cake yarn, wipe frames,*
*sweep floors, untangle bobbins. That's what*
*you do, take what comes along, splinters*
*off the floor, and dirt, lint, and slubs.* —One
was the lace-trimmed, pearl-buttoned
daughter of textile mill profits
until the Depression. —One salvaged
scraps of cotton twill, sewed piecework,
collected bags and bags of buttons. —Which
makes the best story? —*Interlace the yarns,*
*the untwisted or partially twisted fibers,*
*and lock them in place to make a textile.*

—The Fates spin yarns: one winds,
one draws out the thread, one cuts it.
—*Takes special hands for fancy. Harder
to do, but you make more on it.* —If
a thread breaks, you have to tie it up.
—*Rhythm of weaver and loom
makes up a material's lyric structure.*
—*When we make Osnaburg from
floor sweepings, you can see splinters
in the cloth.* —Warp your frame. Draw
threads through the drop-wire harness.
—*You reach high for the big spools
to put on this frame. It runs into a bin
to run the warping to the weave room.*
—All these women, tangled
grandmothers, daughters, mothers.
—Find a pattern. The way you draw it
is the way the cloth comes out. —*Maybe
a thousand to twenty-thousand ends
in the whole pattern. Drawing threads
finer than your own hair.* —Weave any
fabric. Think of the spider. Or don't.
Don't think, like the spider. Spin.

# Technique

Anchor point threaded to
a frame point, then a bridge.

Frame joined, now spokes
for pivoting through sticky

spiral to centering hub.
Then the wait for something

to land, relinquish. So fine
is your radius of cross-

stitched glue, each night's
hunting wears it threadbare;

each morning you must
swallow the dregs. Yes,

of what you've produced.
You feed on your own

shopworn paths. The taste
is bitter and tangled but

placental rich, and you
keep that first bridge

line intact, a wisp of
syntax suspended—

nascent embroidery
to scaffold, fix

onto the moment
something in it

trembles.

# You Never Speak of Anesthesia

Ovoids slipping through conveyor
belts, fallopian tubes, cloacal
chutes, each way variously sorted,
some siphoned, some cartoned,

some discarded. While you were
still mothering, your uterus dropped.
They scooped the spongy tangle
out and stitched you back up.

You never speak of anesthesia.
Blurred white coats gathered like
engorged thunderheads. The heavy
milk of let-down. If you still feel

phantom kicks, flutters—nothing
but gas bubbles. Newborn grimaces,
*ahs* and *oohs* and infant suckles
tossed, along with the plump cheeks

of apple peels, eggshells, melon rinds,
into the compost pile. The birthmarks
now worn into you. Your button bag.
Your lace scraps. Your hands arthritic

from hemming our homemade
dresses. You keep us sewed tight
with firm stitches, white-flour biscuits,
chicken fried in the galley kitchen

you rarely let us enter. You save
old wrapping paper in a shoe box,
cellophane tape folded precisely
back onto itself, torn edges trimmed

with sewing scissors. You crack eggs
on a knife's edge, serve us plates of
sunny-side up with, sometimes, tingeing
the golden yolks, knots of bloodstain.

## Our Lady of Roses

She gave permission. Let us bleed
ourselves more freely. Kim, queen

of the 8th grade, who every month
flooded out her bell-bottom jeans, tied

a borrowed shirt around her waist,
and went about her way. She flaunted

her blossoming, tossing grins askance
through hell-bent curls. Such flirtation,

dirty fertility, that righteous coming
of age again and again. Each minute

all over the world, another egg, another
menses. A new realm of possibilities

brims. It's a story I savor as lushness
condenses, drops from the stem. Have

mercy. Let us pray. Watch over those
who, night and day, toil bodily. Who/

however, wherever you are, may you
be fed, unscathed, and fully worded.

May you know the tiles and tissues
of indoor plumbing. May you seek

all, fear nothing. May you forever
hail your bloody Marys, always

wearing your own glory be.

## Starting with a Diagnosis of Dupuytren's Contracture

In the continent
of my left hand, Vikings land,
stockpile collagen as weapon,
fortress, route—an invasion
of crows' clawed caws—
my dominant, my
writing hand, prey to be,
scavengers' roost of closed-
mouth words falling out of
hand over hand-me-down to
one sleight of or the other—
while sun-sharp shadows
move with the tight fist
of a clock hand—
a second hand, his hand
on my hand on the last
beer in the cooler. So
young then, I was pinned
by the flat of his eyes,
my fingers melted
open to icy numbing no
mere object could object to—
no more me there than
a sponge on a porch railing
soaking up summer's
bellying heat. Brigand,
possessed of brute force
and brilliant ruthlessness—
Baron Guillaume Dupuytren—
Napoleon of surgeons—
1831—first dissected
with transverse incision
a wine merchant's knotted
paw to straighten the fingers—
declared himself namesake

of the disease bullying
my mother's lineage
like a mean drunk, a
one-way clank valve
to the cramped, the
clenched, the broken
compass of the party's
over's stale beer fumes
and no ride home
from okay, whatever
you say like it's any
secret this palmed
someday, my abject
needle threaded
then needlessly,
despite me.

# Childhood Game

Squeeze a tight fist, slowly open
the hand palm up. Stroke down each

finger to the center, the metacarpus,
the Plain of Mars. From there, pull

out an invisible thread that cinches
the fingers together to a slub, a gnarl.

# Committal

Lord how my hand shakes making up
a self I say is mine applying what keeps me
uplifted upright my brushes swabs sponges
absorbing the smell of me that is the smell
of my mother and grandmothers beneath
their powders perfumes odor of the body
thinning extruded by a dim beyond
beyond our undertakings. I touch death

at every wake my fingers compelled
by the cool tallow of flesh the varicose
veining of the road from flatware
to elsewhere. Twilight means time
to draw the curtains. Time is dishwater
dull and dingy like families a squabble
of seagulls that endless seasonal
cycle constant until it wasn't. When

it's time bury me deep in the flood tide
of our bodies scrimshawed over beds books
reading with dogs alongside shedding fleas
flies ticks in the melting squirm and press
of family as herd as pack as extended
appendages for hair brushing lotion
spreading leg shaving back scratching zit
picking pinching tweezering merciless

teasing endless lecturing naked dailiness
of cousins aunts mother grandmother shared
talcum puffs dusting raw underarms spindly
crotches breasts buttocks bony pendulous
supple sagging over belly bulge and stork-like
lifting leg by leg to dip into rivulets of panty
-hose sinuous lipsticked cigarette smoke before
church before God or anyone else dared look.

# Survey of Worker Engagement

Dust so fine we couldn't see it. We coughed a lot.
They said we could go home. We said no, we couldn't lose time.
We just went and learned it with our whole body.
The steam engine turned a wheel high as the top floor.

They said we could go home. We said no, we couldn't lose time.
We danced. We picketed. We paraded.
The steam engine turned a wheel high as the top floor.
Were you working in the mills when ____?

We danced. We picketed. We paraded.
We could stand in the opening and look down in there.
Were you working in the mills when ____?
Our hand slipped. Gears crushed and tore out our thumb.

We could stand in the opening and look down in there.
We found one limb in one place, one in another.
Our hand slipped. Gears crushed and tore out our thumb.
We were always getting caught in the loom.

We found one limb in one place, one in another.
The shuttle flew out and hit us in the head.
We always got caught in the loom
when we tied the ends and went to start it up.

The shuttle flew out and hit us in the head.
Our apron caught in the spinning shaft, threading us in.
We tied the ends on this one and went to start it up.
Our bones snapping as the machine whirled us tighter and tighter.

Our apron caught in the spinning shaft, threading us in
until we jammed the shaft and shut down the works.
Our bones snapping as the machine whirled us tighter and tighter.
Someway that thread wrapped round our finger.

We jammed the shaft to shut down the works.
We were just dust and lint. We coughed a lot.
Someway that thread wrapped round our finger.
Our whole body went in.

II.

## Storm Season

As the season spins up a tangle
of words, look what comes charging,
bucking and snorting. Tell me, old

quarrels, how is this going? Raw
material for millions to make
more millions for a favored few.

Do you understand the dead
are gathering? A sub-verse *sotto
voce* harvest of voices, votes:

evidence of a storm, an atmospheric
system of domestic—I almost wrote
*labor*. Maybe that's because I was

lulled to the tune of a tornado.
It trilled the way my mother could
whistle arias (*Tosca, Madame*

*Butterfly, La Traviata*), conjuring
opera houses out of housework.
But not that day in a vernacular

clapboard two-over-two, no
cellar, no wall without windows.
I'm the newborn bundle

pinched in her arms as
the twister hitches toward us,
furrowed, fluted, determined to

shake our sticky hands, kiss our
sour infants, cyclone-wire our
fields with likely candidates.

Such open-throated perennials.
As if we knew how to stop it,
the baby who keeps on crying.

## Her 1833 testimony on working conditions for children . . . *

If you were Ellen Hooton,
you'd be called a *notorious liar*,
not to be trusted. You'd start

at 5:30 a.m., work until
8:00 p.m. with two breaks.
You'd work in a room with

mostly other children. Just
seven, you are of the youngest,
a piecer at the throstles. You

spend your days reknotting
torn threads as they are
pulled onto the bobbin of

the mule. Only seconds
for each repair, the machine
whirls so fast—all but

impossible to keep up. Too
often your ends are down.
You are beaten by the boss—

your head is *sore with his
hands*. Your mother calls you
*a naughty, stupid girl*, begs

the boss to keep you on so
she doesn't lose your wages.
When you are late to work,

you must walk up and
down the factory floor
with a 20-pound weight

tied around your neck.
Other workers taunt you.
You fall down *several*

*times while fighting*
for your life, fighting
*with a stick*. You

wouldn't think
we'd still be fighting
after all these years.

* before the Central Board of His Majesty's Commissioners, England,
helped propel the updating of the Factory Acts and the regulation of
child labor.

## Shift Work

Those years I chopped steel ties with an ax
to open bales. Dust got so thick one spark

*A bell would ring and let you know*

would ignite the room. It's a fact a burning bale
cannot easily be extinguished. Cotton packed

*you had so much time to eat or sleep*

so tight no force of water can penetrate. That's
why we worked separate from the rest

*or smoke, day or night, on or off your*

of the mill. But cotton and combustion
by God were created through the singeing of

*shift. The mill run regular then. They'd*

angels. The night the mill burned was a Sunday
and the scouring agent was God himself

*blow a whistle for lunch, for break, for*

restless without his servants chopping bales.
Heavenly bolts sparked a firestorm. Flames

*changing out lines. If the whistle blew*

leapt in hallelujahs, racing down shafts
and belt boxes clear through to the engine room.

*otherwise, there'd been an accident. You*

*worried over who might die. You prayed*

> The explosion cracked the roof open, raining
> fiery brimstone on the upper floor, collapsing

*the bell would ring for quitting time. When*

> it to the fourth floor, splitting joists so all
> that wreckage tottered on the gutted remains

*they put clocks on every line, regular time*

> of lower levels like a train wreck hanging off
> a trestle. A sight righteous as Judgment Day,

*meant nothing. If your machines weren't*

> though I never saw it for myself. I'd already
> been laid off, my lungs too cotton-gagged to

*running, you made nothing. You ate smoke,*

> keep time with mill whistles. After the fire,
> might as well be bedridden, nobody working then.

*you slept standing. You stopped worrying*

> *about who'd died. Your shift was running,*

Whole town dried up. Now I mark my breathless
days by the tick of sun along the curtain edges.

> *running the machines until they broke or*

Back when I could still chop, there'd be a tin
bucket on a post. I'd use the dipper to knock

                                *you broke. Day and night, day after day,*

the lint back. If I was between bales, I'd try to
drink soon as they brought the bucket in, before

                                 *whistles blew, bells chimed. For years it's*

lint dust clogged the water so thick it was
like swilling ash of what was to come.

                                 *how it went. It was only a matter of time.*

On breaks, we'd collect quartz rocks. They
said a shoebox full would buy a pocket watch.

## Deathbed Confession

We try to do right by what we love,
what we've worked hard for.

Ever have yellow jackets ground-nest
in the yard, where your kids play?

Then you know. You do what it takes
to rid them. A slug of gasoline,

fire in the hole—how my daddy taught me.
Those commie yanks setting up camp,

riling the workers, they were the disease,
we were just the fever. That night,

I couldn't say what made me grab
my wife's hosiery. Things unfolding

too fast to find a meal sack or scissors,
and there they were on the chair—

the stockings that held Addie's thighs
on Sundays. I doubled one inside

the other, pulled them over my head.
—If a belt snaps on a spinning mule,

you got to shut it down. An accordion
press of nose stump, lip flaps, eye slits

erased me from the mirror. At
the meet up, it was hard to see much

past the mask's fleshy weave but other
masks flinging hatchets, pick axes,

sledgehammers. We didn't kill anyone.
We just broke up the nest. Smashed in

windows, hacked up filing cabinets,
tables and chairs, ripped open every bag

of flour and rice, dropped poison
in the well, doused all the rubble left

of union headquarters in kerosene
and lit it on fire. I caught hell from

Addie when I got home for laddering
up her Sunday stockings, a smoky mess

she threw in the trash. But I held her
close and promised her new ones.

I took another job. We moved out
west, ducked the next acts that

addled the South—circus of strikes,
murders, rigged juries, mistrials

blacklists, bankruptcies, and then
the whole big cotton tent collapsing.

But what I told no one till now is
how I never saw my face again

as others regard it. Instead,
mirrors show me swollen jowls

squeezed up like sausage in casing,
rotten sausage with maggots in it.

I see my kids back-when, monkeying
in the car, smearing their foreheads

and lips on the window glass, stuck
that way. I see the smoldering lump

of ash rising from the front page
photograph in the paper that morning.

It's taken years of old age for the mask
everyone views as me to melt into

my real face, the rancid rayon mesh
my tongue bumps at for bits of corn mush.

You see it, I can tell. But do you also
smell it? The kerosene? Strong fumes still.

Take a whiff. That's the smell of love,
my friend, striking the first match.

# Linthead Stomp

"mill workers dancing during strikes to bolster solidarity and block mill entrances"
—*The Voice of Southern Labor: Radio, Music, and Textile Strikes, 1929-1934*

We dance in shifts :: We dance in waves ::
Angels clogging :: In flying squadrons ::
We dance against the :: Stretch out ::
We dance for :: A living wage ::
We dance to stop :: Watch :: Us dance ::
On tables :: On graves :: We dance ::
In aprons :: In rollers :: We dance ::
On principle :: We dance ::
The time :: Away :: We whirlwind ::
Entry :: Block your spindle maze ::
We are :: Spinning girls ::
Prance machines :: You can't ::
Catch us :: Bossman :: We are ::
Full snarls :: Sharp teeth :: We comb ::
Clean sweeps :: We turn gears ::
Inside :: Out :: We are hooves ::
Pawing :: We are :: Just ::
Getting started :: For you ::
We dance :: To hell on wheels ::
You can't stand to :: Watch us ::
You call us :: Killing whirls :: You ::
Call us :: Carcass pickers :: Criminals ::
We dance all :: Which and anyways ::
Just keep your :: Head down so ::
You don't have to :: Watch ::
The kill in :: Progress ::
You can't :: Stop it :: You say ::
We can't :: Last :: Just watch us ::

# Labor

*We leave our homes in the morning,*
*We kiss our children goodbye . . .*
> —"The Mill Mother's Lament,"
> Ella May Wiggins, d. Sept. 14, 1929

*Lord a-mercy, they done shot*
*and killed me*—her last words
some say. Picture her seven-

months pregnant, legs dangling
from back of the flatbed,
stirring up exhaust, the striker-

packed truck turned away,
forced back, the union rally
receding in grind and rattle,

dust and gravel and potholed
sweat, the clammy fabric of
their shirts, her dress—breast-

bones, armpits—loosening
with air. You could say they're
on a lark, an outing, and not be

far wrong. Charley unpockets
a tin harmonica; another striker
hawk-spits to clear his throat.

Acceleration carries them
from their voices; their quavers
tangle in tree limbs like cobwebs

broken and trailing, netting
insect carapaces, stray bits.
Four ragged crows follow,

crying *Mama,* her four babies
dead of pertussis. *My sweets,*
*what brings you nigh? Mama,*

*we come to hear you.* The child
in her flutters as if to join them.
She lays hand to her belly. *Hush.*

Lint-flecks sift from her hair,
dandelion fluff seeding. *Hush*
*now. Hear me sing.* She spins

her rich alto as though it could
barricade the road with thick
webbing, protect the strikers

in the truck, feed her hungry
children at home, keep us safe
from ourselves. You could say

she sees what is coming. She
says, *Younguns, you must go.*
The birds caw and wheel

off the way time always flies
us to a tense imperfect future,
which here means carloads

of union busters, armed
and pursuing collision—labor
obstructed being somehow

cheaper than giving berth.
The truck driver can't brake
quickly enough. Thrown

from the flatbed, Ella May
leans against a side rail,
dazed in the bright sun of

September's goldenrod
and gun fire. The shot burns
into her, wet and cold.

As she gargles on her own
blood, Charley stays, holds
her, holds the stilled egg

sack of their never-born.
Others run, and who's to
say we aren't also running,

won't always be running
naked, wailing, and raw
with want? Who's to say

we're not all still pouring
from her opened chest
in clamorous swarms—

# The Tornado Nursery, or Working the Stretch-Out

I start dreaming

of tornadoes.
Skinny ones, fat ones. White
ones, gray ones, scorch black

carving open ground.
                              Some
span the town, some worm

through crooks and crannies

or finger in furrows. Some glower
and stomp like the shift boss.
Some rage up wordless.
                              I call

for my children to shelter
in ditch or shed—but they

always scatter, flighty chicks

I can't catch hold of. Fists of air,
loose feathers.
                    Days I shuttle looms,

work my worries into cloth.
Come home with nothing
                              but

my voice to soothe my younglings,
cocoons I'd first spun
inside me,

each raw hint wheeling
into clay

knobs
of heels, noggin, rump bones.

I feed them
as I can—gusts, key shifts,
strands of rain—

    but one by one they

thin, knuckle over
to formless lumps.

Air stales with their dried sputum.
Their wheezes eddy to dust

no matter how much I rock

or how
long I sing. Yard by yard my

heart unravels.

    Now fields are bare,
the mills shut down. I brood

on husks—split cicada casings,
unswaddled clumps of batting,

I call their names

to raise a chorus.
What I make

is not a sound.

# General Strike

I declare a strike.
I protest each body
lowered to join others
in the ground. I protest
bodies ravaged in fields,
mines, factories, in all
the world's minefields.
I protest the ravaged
plains, mountains, forests,
seas. I protest the ravages
of time in my own body,
indignities as yet only
to my vanity, trivial
in light of these other
ravagings but still, I
must confess, deeply
felt. Because I once
knew well the stages
of labor and delivery,
I protest the ways
I've been woven into
the warp and weft of
history, bound by its
threads as tightly as
insect prey in a web,
gagged, paralyzed by
my own inertia. I will
now will my flailing
to resolve into a flicker
on the radar, a clog
in the gears, a dry
womb insistently,
inconceivably
quickening.

III.

# Where Dollars Are Born,
## or Regarding the Rotary Digester

First you see the rafters strung
with iron ornaments. It looks pretty
crazy, all these colossal globs of
ore skirting the cross beams like
steam-addled pressure cookers. Is
it crazy to forge the cost of beauty?
By now you see how alarmingly we
hang from such heights in our ball
gowns. At first, we were steaming
mad, dressing under pressure, so
much silk taffeta to iron, so many
wrought buttons hanging by threads.
But we do look fetching dressed
up for the party and swinging like
barbells. We are something else,
you see. We are busy inside this
cast iron. We are onto something.
Call it a kind of parboiling of fast
cash, assets acid-etched from
intestinal depths. Call it billows
of digestion. Call it irony. Call us
butterflies, if you must. Call on
iron chefs and obstetricians to
deliver a last meal of champagne
and beaten biscuits, as flashing
disco balls spit wads of new
currency at the ceiling and walls.
You'll say it's a steep price to
pay, but that's the vertiginous
splendor of industry. It makes
you dizzy to look up and see us
hanging there, pretty razor-wired
cocoons undressed by gravity.

# Bankrolled, or Cotton Money

Like magic, the first cash you withdrew
—the ATM slot spitting out stacked bills
in the middle of the night in the middle of
nowhere without the touch of another hand.
Which enabled you to buy that extra ounce
to snort and keep raring until dawn. Rolling
a tube with the freshest, stiffest bill. Using
that weevil implement to inhale bits of fiber
and dye residue with the drug, circulate its
currency through your whole body. Vintage
commerce. You'll never be that virgin again

because who carries cash anymore? Cotton
fibers beaten to cloth then packed/packaged
to vanquish/salvage the Grand Old South.
Fibers pulped and boiled to a slurry with
molecules of soils, weevils, molds, muscle
and joint aches dragged row after row into
gunny sacks. Fiber-woven paper minted
to keep all that past intact, wash after
wash, as cellulose absorbs water and jam-
packed bills come through the machine wet

but holding up under wear and tear, like
a twenty you forgot in the back pocket of
the jeans you were folding from laundry
basket to dresser drawer. The gift of extra
cash, cotton unfolded from fold and seam.
The eventual machines and chemicals
displacing/releasing all those bodies from
the fields. Running up historical endnotes
on the watermarked/-logged souls left
footing and shouldering and still holding
the bill. What saved your sorry cotton-

tail ass? You skinny embossed linen, you
ink-blotted rag, your fine stationary hitting
a nerve like a squalling infant's fisted and
snotty outrage. Your eye bruised in birth,
your grandparents' cook washed and prayed
you clean at the kitchen sink in the spatter
of fried chicken grease, upholding you
to the roar of the spigoted baptismal font.
His name was Luther. You came through
wet but intact—healed, in fact, your blessed
tissues leached of pigment. He laid hands
on the black eye you were born with—what

was the cost of that? How many dog-eared
flanneled dollars counted from white palms
into his? Luther saved up his cotton in worn
sheets, picking, cooking, preaching, cleaning
enough to pay for a righteous burial. When
the cotton ran out, he learned how to raid his
capital. When that ran out, he learned how
bad credit stimulates an economy. He learned
it was a proven fact that cotton money rolls
over when money runs out of cotton. Follow
fiber through the network. Access kitchens,
bed- and bathrooms, closets through fiber

optics. For service, ring this bell. To play,
press enter. Watching, listening in—addictive
uptake from confidential sources. To strike
a nerve, press on the machine. Press into
your own eye sockets. To print, first save
your work then push this button. To stimulate
the economy, print this sanctioned text onto
the clean surfaces of proprietary cotton paper.
Fibers absorb the ink in a series of baths. You

are awash in fresh web applications. Online
and born again. Look harder. It's all there:
hands pressed into your skin, savings earned
to be heard, years of compounded interest.

## "Nearby Super-Earth Likely a Diamond Planet"

*—Science Daily*


Since you've discovered in this milky way
a planet of diamond, you've been obsessed:

A whole carbon-pressed world. A planet that can
cut glass, conduct heat and crystalline sound.

Our estimated value: $26.9 nonillion, according
to your forbes.
                Our eyes are the jeweler's glasses

of god. We read meaning into the smallest irregularities,
in interior gleam. Walking in fullight is something

we're taught to avoid, emerging only when the sunstar
fades from the polished facetlands and rocky

commerce starts humming.
                        You can't
possibly leave it alone, now that you know

what we're made of. All you could want, more
than you ever dreamed of. You imagine tunneling

in, scraping out glittering geological excrement.
You'll find it isn't the light that damages but what you

see: the insights. So bright everything else is invisible.
There are consequences
                to love.

You believe anything can be possessed
with the right instruments: attitude, luck, longing,

all compressed until hard as diamond, which
means "proper," "unalterable," "unbreakable,"

but also "I overpower," "I tame." It isn't brilliance
that burns in you. It isn't light
                              that guides you.

# A Supposition of Spider Goats

Suspended in a field of yellow silk stronger than Kevlar:

a golden orb weaver spider in Madagascar. Anything
else so silkily engineered would be armored. So, what if

a *solution from one field can solve problems in completely
different fields?* White-coated researchers round up orb
spiders for milking, each *Nephila* snared with gauze,

*the dragline tugged from her abdomen and wound
around a spindle.* Then what's the problem? Problem is

they are small; their production is low; they are territorial
and cannibalistic. That's where the goats come in.
Test subjects implanted with spider silk—*teats equal*

*spinnerets*—silk proteins processed out like skimming
*curds from whey.* And then a thousand spindles drone like

the inside of a hornet's nest, shuttles slamming transgenic
picker-sticks for *a better means of mass-production,*
materials with *toughness and modulus of elasticity—an ability*

*to stretch without breaking.* Which means more security,
more protection. We're right on the money tuffet. We can grow

insatiable monsters all in a row. When the goats lactate,
their silky sulky fibers twist into effluents of milky green.
(Imagine the plugged ducts, mastitis fever dreams conjuring

*goat-sized spiders with a taste for human flesh* that smash
all tuffets and frighten Miss Muffet away.) Meanwhile,

Old Joe's been milking his spider goats for a few years now.
Their udders hold promise. He hopes one day to cultivate
spider cotton, maybe spider alfalfa. He's determined, invested,

and thinking big. But let's return to armed forces and skin
that's bulletproof. Could we finally be safe from fire's arms,

brands, sales, storms? Or at least finely bespoke our own
performance pieces? (A biotech artist implants the material
in vitro in human skin, titles the project *2.6g 329m/s* for

the weight and velocity of a .22 caliber slug, the industry
standard for Type I bulletproof vests. The sample stops

some bullets fired in slow-mo, none shot at full speed. That
nothing is safe is an ancient truth. One we must, apparently,
keep relearning.) Back on Joe's farm, our amber-eyed piece

-work pastorals frolic in the field, unaware a competitor
emerges, boding obsolescence: hagfish, as it turns out—

a protein exuded in the primordial *what ifs* of their slime.

## Dear Cotton:

You are in my blood.
My sweetheart, my fiberfill,
fierce white, pure red, the scent

of ice, fire, and survival.
I couldn't wait for the first
smear, rustier than I'd

supposed, but opening to
vermilion. Rose petals splashed
across crotch, leaking through

layers while you swabbed,
staunched, padded, buffered,
offered me tampon as pen

to scrawl toilet bowl
graffiti, clots of my unborn,
scabbed over indelible shadows,

phantom stains dim in the fabric.
Honey, you've absorbed enough
years of my runoff to know

the funds are drying up.
I want a few more bouquets,
a last-ditch burial, and your

instructional diagram
girl, leg hiked up akimbo,
to guide me through.

# Thread Count

This is a thread of love.
Or is it a threat of love?
Are you a carpet, a sari,
a scarf, a sanitary pad,
a set of napkins, a work
shirt, a pair of trousers,
yet another goddamned
useless throw pillow?
Let's keep blowing kisses.
A shit storm is accruing
in the model forecasts.
A poor dusty cricket drags
a cracked back leg, aching
to stridulate. This, too, is
a type of sewing, another
kind of story. More lands
strip-searched for stuff,
steeped in a moonlight
of insecticide. Hear how
the drone of working
conditions wheels from
steeples to shafts to
spindles to sweatshops
to now some bloodless
beyond. Ever more
brilliant, our artificial
illuminations. Just think
how the nights once burst
at the seams with stars,
the air gauzy with their
errant garments, our naked
awe tightly plied with lust.

# In a fever pitch, machines

concentrate high-paid
waste, incinerating

for the choir. New
forms hum to aged anger,

steeped and wide and deep.
I want to quit all this.

I want to swim in my own
school of wildfire with

a heavenly smile.
In this sponge baptism

of heat, who wouldn't
believe in bacteria, in

the viscous characters we
meet in thickets and by-

ways, the symptomatic
faiths stewing in red clay,

cultivating pipelines
of wiregrass headaches.

I've bagged my share
of infectious myth,

morals of gas leaks
instead of legal

needle exchange. If I
stay put, I can stay

clean. If I go, I'll just go
back to the same old

songs my mama's mama
sang the day they dared

her to walk a bed of
live coals in her bare feet

and she did.

# Harvest Song I

It's official: cotton vagina has been
debunked. But further aridities persist.
The climate has questions, as do I. About
the way we poison rivers. About the way
we pray. So the king could experience

for himself a bountiful harvest, workers
were ordered to reattach to stems all
the white tufts they had just labored
to pick. Some applied drops of glue
inside the bolls. Some delicately

pressed the fibers on and secured
the cotton capsules to their stalks.
Others swept the main road with
fresh-cut pine boughs to keep it
clean. Meanwhile the king crashed

through a farm gate, truck careening
into a field, hitting a thicket. His high
-ness took off running. He bolted. He
bailed. Because the world has entirely
too much cotton. Enough for hundreds

of billions of tee shirts, but hardly
enough to bandage all the backs on
which our crops and countries were
grown. And our growth metastasized.
To fight the war on breast cancer, we

can now Kickstart cotton baled in pink
plastic wrap. Have ourselves a field day.
You crave more of this luscious weather?
There are other rackets that don't
flush us down the drain, other weeds

making legal waves. Next hot growing
season, give edibles a try. Until then,
let's stop shooting off our cannon
mouths with moths to carpet bomb
other pests. I believe in the questions

to many answers. Well, sort of. It all
gets a bit fuzzy. Somewhere, rivers
run fluorescent green, purple, orange,
stocked with resistant insects. But rest
assured, our vaginas are in the clear.

IV.

# Harvest Song II

*—Except genetically modified cotton
is resistant to glyphosate.* Sprayed
on open buds, glyphosate condenses
and soaks in: 85% of personal
hygiene products are contaminated.
*—Bloom and fade, the flowers sing.*
A mascara tube or shampoo bottle must
litany its ingredients. Not so a box
of tampons. *—Secure a staunch of
cotton-wool to a rod and gently insert
until it reaches the neck of the womb.*
A lifetime of washing my red stains
from white sheets. *—Sometimes they
cause pain; sometimes they are of evil
colour and not according to nature;
sometimes strange things stream forth
from within.* If only we could return
through the dim hole of our first days.
*—Set into place, and the rod withdrawn.*
Back through rendezvous and roofs
and resurrections. Shadows of mothers
and fathers in adjacent rooms. Swirls
of Rorschach inks in draining waters.
*—Sometimes they flow by drops, or
overflow. They sometimes flow too soon,
sometimes too late, or are quite stopt
that they flow not at all.* My first time,
I followed the illustrated instructions,
plump curves of vulva labia vagina,
into which I inserted soft nesting
material. *—Sing of the flowers that
bloom and fade without regret.* Before
the cotton bolls, the petals unfurl
white or pink. Uterus after uterus. All
our blossoms in the trash deposited.

Our known and unknown losses until
the batting begins to pill and molt.
—*Weave not in memory's cloth these
days gliding into night.* What leaks
then is the bladder of memory. Elixir
of cotton-petal flavonoids, a new drug
for memory loss enters clinical trials.
Gauzy promises of cures, a distant
woof to maybe stave circling wolves.
—*Take these threads and weave
upon your loom a fabric* of centuries
and multitudes. The revolving door
to a trading floor once bustling with
merchants and littered with lint is
chained shut. Can this be the end
of a story that has fathomed me
so long and so deeply? Flowers
and flower songs disappear into
a dark beyond regret, ushered by
the beveled end of a speculum.

# Textiloma

*Also gossypiboma, gauzoma, muslinoma, cottonoid. Textiles still in the body after the body has been incised and sutured by surgical knife and needle. Left behind by accident. An oversight, usually in procedures abdominal, gynecological. Cotton matrix breeding granuloma. Inflammatory reaction to an abscess maybe, maybe adhesion.*

Think of the unintended consequences of every-
thing you've ever opened yourself up to. Foreign
bodies in dark places, corners, cavities. Sometimes
after months, or years they migrate. A restlessness

within. Gauze, sponge, towel, swab become egg,
incandescent bulb, bull-headed skull. Blunt ovoid
bumping up against ordinary workings of stomach
and bowels, drumming on membranes. Hair ball

coughed up by exploratory laparoscopy. Sprouted
onion, lewd fungus, nudging blunthead. A slip of
the tongue, that language placenta. Or a pearl,
of course a pearl, gathering irritation around it

like a shawl, a crochet afghan, snug against hard
weather. Moth web-lodged in the porch eaves.
Beached breach of barnacle-encrusted, sonar-
haunted whale. Insomniac with transistor radio

tucked under pillow, late-night talk show hosts
whispering obituaries in your ear—
                          Sometime
after 2 a.m. you give up sleep for a fit of laundry,
are startled by a monster swaying midair in front

of you, what is actually an eastern hercules beetle
lumbering up in its misplaced nuptial flight at
the bare-bulbed dawn of basement light. Later
you find the beetle bladdered in a fetid scum

of crumbled concrete, dryer lint, and shed dog
hair, oaring through thick periphery, winding
down to dry up behind the back leg of the tool
bench. Squalid mausoleum for such heroic

impotence. Not how we imagine ourselves
arriving and leaving here—
                            Attenuated, desiccated,
diminished. Unforeseen, unbeknownst. Crumpled
tissue tossed into hydraulic darkness, only to
resurface as sodden shreds clinging to clothes
you lift from the washer. Chrysalis corpse. How
else does the body say *I'm tired, I'm bored, I'm
lost* so you recognize the residue, the aroma?

# Grisaille

## I.

Maybe a cow is calving somewhere.
Maybe someone is dying, is sick of ease,
is hungry for adventure, justice, freedom

beyond tasseled trim. But on these toile
drapes, figures work at playing catch, at
swinging on planks hung from generous

tree limbs, at fiddling, feasting, waltzing.
He extends his hand, she tilts a reciprocal
cheekbone. Light outlines their edges. They

launch into a tidy spin among sheaf, barrel,
bench. Two goats hunker, knuckle-kneed.
A piebald dog antics for scraps. Their

patterned days repeating, repeating,
repeating. Somewhere there must be
consequences. But I can't find any.

Downbow to gavotte. Patterned shadows
dance to the tune of pewter, carbon, cinder,
and fog. The famished dog begs to differ.

## II.

I'm good at it because I don't wear gloves.
I start with flatware and serving utensils.
Move on to shine salt cellars and bread plates.

Then I muscle vases, goblets, Revere bowls
and carving platters in the corner cabinets.
These are larger, more oxidized, take at

least two rounds of rubbing paste and rinsing.
From dense sideboard innards: stored urns,
water pitchers, gravy boats, tiered dessert stands,

chafing dishes, an heirloom repoussé punch
bowl to serve twenty, each piece blinding
by the time I'm finished. I'm also skilled

at cleaning toilets. Scrub porcelain meticulously
free of rust stains, mucus and clot spatter,
shed hairs, flecks of crusted shit, congealed

piss, sometimes vomit, stray fungused toenail
clippings. It takes bare hands, contact with actual
skin. Takes, you could say, an intuitive musing

of fingertips to appreciate nuances in patinas.
To feel out intricacies of relief. To comprehend
something—anything—of price, privilege.


III.

In the space between toile and toil lurk
our chronic hungers. Somber specters
of dove, oyster, silver, gunmetal, granite,

soot, charcoal, ash, dust. Surround dark
with light: the dark appears darker.
Surround light with dark and the light

is blighted. Maybe love subsists on
monochrome—our gray-mattered words,
their afterburn. Van Gogh wrote to Theo

that colors are but spectrums of grayscale—
red-gray, yellow-gray, blue-gray, green-gray,
orange-gray, violet-gray. *All one really*

*sees are those tones and shades.* It's
the dead layer of underpainting that creates
the illusions we crave of depth and our

animal luminosity. Except I can't see
past shabby valances, exhausted paint,
tarnished ghosts. Once I was young

and starved enough to carve "LOVE"
deep into the thin muslin of my inner
wrist. I drew blood, fed scars. Howling

now outside the frame is a bigger picture.
Consequences leaking accelerants of oil
and rage. The drapes dancing with flames.

# Field Study / Search Field

maybe in the first fluff-pocked scrub trees
precursor tufts prickled with coarse hairs

littered through with intractable seeds we'd
find words for the matter at hand the fabric

afoot come to raw fiber washed clean beaten
on a mat combed into strands to twist into

thread fine as sunlight she rubbed spider
webs on her arms and hands never tired

of weaving bolts of the commonplace to
lay over the faces of the dead simple as

rain and wind present as haptic worlds
flitting at the twig ends of our neurons

before we turn merchant and mill so you'd
like to think they who led these vegetable

lambs to the yarn's yawning orifice who
find spandex an intimate tissue between

arbor and ardor would that there were so
many words for the same blank screen

used to pay tribute and taxes on skinny
seedling stock too much rain the days

infected with root rot unproductive small
cup cotton bra full coverage pesticide news

in Chihuahua Rep. Cotton says something
dumb sign up at Cotton Top this Sunday

to give a rescue pet a home in the fabric
of our lives incorporated cotton dust

and field-dried bract extract in rat lungs
nearby in the same cotton field were found

the bodies of five more tiny brown
flecks in the fabric are natural leaf stem

and seed remnants not 800 thread count
hotel luxury sheets but GMO plants

in the refuge where Bt-sensitive worms
mate with impervious worms to water

down resistance traits victims in this case
were young underprivileged women

workers students the future of sustainable
agriculture smells earthy musty abducted

upland plants produce creamy buds that
bloom in a day or two by morning flowers

turn a pinkish hue that indicates pollination
proof has been accepted that they suffered

physical ill-treatment likely sexual abuse
before shedding petals within a week bolls

set as they say in the field yellow-white red
then dead eight pink crosses in the field

in the case of *Cotton Field* the findings we
have determined smallholder farms this

season latest estimates suggest the pattern
and profusion of cellulose growth until a boll

opens fiber is a living cell meanwhile inside
dark confines the factory is manufacturing

## Beautiful and Uniform

Too often we disappear,
slipped between the pages
of loose lips, kissed to
palimpsests. So much
and nothing is written
between the lines of
our words, fragile as
clavicles. From the end
of a row of looms, you
watch frames churning,
fabrics pouring stark
over rollers. You see who
breathes and births cloth,
becomes cloth, fabric
grown from red clay,
jaundiced rooms, pale
rubble of bone-worn
skin. The remnants of
a light snow almost
gone. Haunting, this wet
weight of laundry wrung
to ribbons, to slipknots
of empty sleeves flapping
on twine against overcast
skies. Monotonous harvest
without our high-strung
voices, our capable hands.

## Dropped Stitch

Many rows along, you realize you've
miscounted. One tug and you're back

to a single thread, except now the yarn
bears the dents, kinks, and frays of

all the stitches you've just unraveled.
You can never unmake these stories.

## Brute Chorus

What's done remains
unproven; still there's
food for the patient

spider. That's the silken
thread of Athena's text.

For Apollo, harrier
of logic and light, it's
totally not. Hard fact

is how humans are
conceived, and, just

as none shall exhaust
the wine-dark sea,
wombs are conspicuous

consumption. He can
tolerate no such mother

-fuckingly crimson
draperied death traps.
Forget the gods. We

stand for mortal skeins.
Penelope has subtle

matter to her, the trick
of the wife threading
through all plots. But

the art that slays it
truly is a fatal robe,

a toxic shirt, a poison
dress (signed Deianira,
Clytemnestra, Medea).

Woven nets of furies.
Substance of women's

work we all reference
and resist; revise, reap,
relentlessly reprieve.

(Thus, this tidal being
born, mired, warped in

blood). How it suits us.

## Less than Last

The river pours in fretwork
cables, iron rainfall rough-
wrought to turning mill wheel.

Heavy hearts and lungs, livelier
eyes seeing less and less than last
year's hard of hearing. Little by

little are we poorer in the fruits
of our labor, churned by machines,
evicted from rooms. We lick

broken thread ends, knot, reset,
weave endless debt. Each stitch
wins us poison for those who in

the name of god I do not blame
aside for their sinning or how
they without drowning swim it.

We're swallowing the earth,
on our knees riding out the brunt
of our own storms. Last things

first in these hospice hours we
brood over, chilling ourselves
calm. We pray it will be okay.

That our children, all beings
will be okay. That instead of
torrents slashing sideways,

the sky falls on us softly,
tenderly, proffered waters
we might sip from spoons.

# What my grandmother knew

in the delivery room, bearing
down on my mother,
small glory crowning
as the mill whistle blew
for noon:

*It's about time.*

# Drawing In

*—threading yarns from a new warp to weave new cloth*

# Reweaving a World, or Dynamic Symmetry

*All life is working towards a state of exaltation.*

*Work is one form of worship.*

—Mary Crovatt Hambidge

First the bleating and tinkling, then the sheep
come nuzzling in with their clear eyes. We'd
rather be one cog in the wheel of truth than

work the whole wheel in a machinery of lies.
Getting to the heart of things isn't reprising
where we started. Between the circle

and the spiral are moments held apart.
We're pauses, dramas born on horizontal
planes to learn, to settle our differences

with fields and herds and all their close
-cropped clearings. We hunger for earth, sky,
tree rings of thought after drought. No clock

can rewind us. Warp cannot escape wolf.
If we can't reclaim the center, why leave to
begin with? —So loss can find. Death gives

us riches: matter disintegrated, absorbed
into darkness, then reconceived, muscling
to musical light—illuminations angled in

clinking sheep bells. We'll relinquish
only to resurge, an explosion poised
on a caesura, threads eternally spinning—

# Notes

Bits of language in many of these poems were adapted from various sources, including the University of North Carolina at Chapel Hill's Center for the Study of the American South and Digital Innovation Lab (Loray Mill Project); child worker Ellen Hooton (1833 testimony on working conditions for children in factories to the Central Board of His Majesty's Commissioners, England); Jacquelyn Down Hall, et al (*Like a Family: The Making of a Southern Cotton Mill World*); Victoria Byerly (*Hard Times Cotton Mill Girls*); Patrick Huber (*Linthead Stomp: The Creation of Country Music in the Piedmont South*); the Mayo Clinic ("Dupuytren's Contracture"); the Southern Textile Industry Project (2000 report on Loray Mill for the *Historic American Engineering Record*, for an erasure poem of sorts); Robert Benincasa ("Where Dollars Are Born," *Planet Money*, NPR); Dutch artist and entrepreneur Jalila Essaïdi; Edson Marchiori, et al. ("Textiloma: A Forgotten Diagnosis"); Rabindranath Tagore (*The Hungry Stones and Other Stories*); seventeenth century midwife Jane Swift (as quoted in S. Read's *Menstruation and the Female Body in Early Modern England*), Ashley Fetters ("The Tampon: A History," *The Atlantic*); Mary Crovatt Hambidge (*Apprentice in Creation*); and innumerable internet searches.

Typically, these bits are indicated by italics; rarely are these borrowings verbatim or used consecutively from the same source text.

# Acknowledgments

Thank you to the editors and staff of the journals in which these poems first appeared, often in different forms and sometimes with different titles, including *The Colorado Review*, *Fourth River*, *Green Humanities*, *Spiral Orb*, *Terrain.org: A Journal of the Built and Natural Environments*, and *Yellow Chair Review*. An earlier version of "Shift Work" was anthologized in *Even the Daybreak: 35 Years of Salmon Poetry*. "Storm Season" appears in *Terrain.org's* anthology, *Letters to America*. "Field Study / Search Field" appears in the Poetry Foundation's video series, *Ours Poetica*. Thank you to Red Bird Chapbooks for publishing *Shift Work*, a limited-edition chapbook that includes early versions of a number of these poems and from which this collection grew. And, of course, thank you to Kevin Watson, to Pam Uschuk and William Pitt Root, and to all of Press 53.

A 2015-16 sabbatical allowed me time for the travel and research that led to these poems. Thank you to all who put me up and put up with me during that time, including Kathy Swain in Rhode Island; Susan Amster and family in Massachusetts; Sel Kardan and family in Los Angeles; Amelia Smith, all the Grays, and the folks at Loray Mill in Gastonia, North Carolina; and, especially, my mom, who was born to the noon mill whistle and is everywhere.

Gratitude to the organizations that have supported me, especially my academic home, Randolph College (formally Randolph-Macon Woman's College) and my colleagues there in the English Department and beyond, including the Maier Museum and Randolph MFA. The Association for the Study of Literature and Environment (ASLE) has long been another home. In 2016, the Hambidge Center's award of the Garland Distinguished Fellowship granted me an incredibly productive residency in those north Georgia mountains. The Daily Grind Writing Series has kept me grinding, and the Star City Ukulele Circle started me strumming. More recently, I'm beyond grateful to the Black Earth Institute and all my amazing fellow fellows, both current and former.

To the following individuals, some near, some far; some teachers, mentors, cheer squad, or friends, or, in few cases, all of the above— thank you: Nancy Allen, Debra Allbery, Mara Amster, Karen Anderson, Scott Cardwell, Anne-Marie Creamer, Gary Dop, Teresa Dzieglewicz, Camille Dungy, Ann Fisher-Wirth (endless thanks and love), Carolyn Forché, Chris Gaumer, jd hegarty, dog Ida, Lisa Kiernan, Grant Kittrell, Aviya Kushner, Cricket Matthews, Rose McLarney, Kathy Muehlemann, Kyle Mundy, Sydna Mundy and Alex Kaplan, Lucy Penegar, Jim Peterson, Ira Sadoff, Harriet Tarlo and Judith Tucker, Ellen Bryant Voigt, Lesley Wheeler, and Fran Wilde. Also, to my grandmothers, who gave me material to weave and buttons to sew.

Finally, and most deeply, thank you to Jay Kardan, who is everything.

Laura-Gray Street is author of *Pigment and Fume* (Salmon Poetry 2013) and *Shift Work* (Red Bird Chapbooks 2016) and co-editor of three anthologies: *The Ecopoetry Anthology* (Trinity University Press 2013), *A Literary Field Guide to Southern Appalachia* (University of Georgia Press 2019), and *Attached to the Living World: A New Ecopoetry Anthology* (Trinity University Press 2025). Her poetry has received prizes from *The Greensboro Review*, the Dana Awards, the Southern Women Writers Conference, *Isotope: A Journal of Literary Science and Nature Writing*, and *Terrain.org: A Journal of the Built and Natural Environments*; published in *The Cider Press Review*, *The Colorado Review*, *Poet Lore*, *Poetry Daily*, *Shenandoah*, *The Notre Dame Review*, *Blackbird*, and elsewhere; and been supported by fellowships from the Virginia Commission for the Arts, the Virginia Center for the Creative Arts, the Artist House at St. Mary's College in Maryland, the Hambidge Center for the Arts and Sciences, where she was the Garland Distinguished Fellow in 2016, and Storyknife. In 2018 her collaboration with UK visual artist Anne-Marie Creamer was on display in galleries in Sheffield, England, and Yantai, China. Street holds an MFA from Warren Wilson and an MA from the University of Virginia. A 2022–2025 fellow with the Black Earth Institute, she is the Mary Frances Williams Professor of English, directs the Creative Writing and Visiting Writers Series Program, and edits *Revolute*, MFA's literary journal, at Randolph College on the unceded traditional lands of the Monacan Indian Nation called Lynchburg, Virginia, beside the James River.

www.ingramcontent.com/pod-product-compliance
Lightning Source LLC
Chambersburg PA
CBHW021509090426
42739CB00007B/535